GRAMMAR COP

Super-fun Reproducible Pages That Give Kids Practice in Parts of Speech, Capitalization, Punctuation, and More!

by the staff of *Storyworks* magazine

NEW YORK • TORONTO • LONDON • AUCKLAND • SYDNEY

MEXICO CITY • NEW DELHI • HONG KONG • BUENOS AIRES

Cover design by Gerard Fuchs
Interior design by Russell Bart
Illustrations by Jack Desroscher

ISBN 0-439-51375-8
Copyright © 2004 by Scholastic Inc.
All rights reserved.
Printed in the U.S.A.

3 4 5 6 7 8 9 10   40   10 09 08 07 06 05 04

Contents

SPELLING & USAGE

Answers

Introduction

Grammar Cop has been one of *Scholastic Storyworks* magazine's most popular features over the years—and now, we've compiled the best of these super-fun grammar activity pages all in one book!

Students will have a blast reading the hilarious adventures of their favorite storybook characters and correcting their mistakes all in the name of the law—grammar laws, that is. They'll enforce the rules of grammar to help the animals in Old MacDonald's farm learn the difference between *we* and *us*, teach Mary's little rooster (not lamb) which verb tense to use, correct the Frog Prince's spelling in his letter of apology to the witch, and much more!

Inside, you'll find 40 reproducible activity pages that give students practice in parts of speech, capitalization and punctuation, contractions, spelling, and usage. You can make an overhead transparency of each activity page and work on it together as a whole class. Or you can distribute copies for students to take home as homework or to work on when they're waiting for the rest of the class to finish their work. These activity pages are perfect for reviewing grammar skills that you've already taught or to assess how much students have learned.

Enjoy!

Name: _____ Date: _____

Nouns

The Case of the Strange Playground Equipment

Build a roller coaster for the school playground? Find out what the Super-Riders Construction Team thinks about this highly unusual request!

Directions: Underline all the nouns in the letter below. Then go back and circle the proper nouns.

Dear Principal Billsley,

It's very unusual for my company to receive a letter like the one you sent. We've never built a roller coaster in a school's backyard before. We're thrilled for the opportunity!

The Super-Riders Construction Team has taken a look at the plans you included with your letter. It's a shame you used a crayon. The ideas you drew on the school picture were hard to read. But we liked what we saw. As you wrote, the second loop will require demolishing the school cook's cafeteria. I hope she won't mind.

Of course, every good roller coaster needs an exciting name. I'm not sure your suggestion, the "Kara Has Cooties Coaster," is appropriate. What about the "Multiplication Shocker" or the "Research Report Terror"? That's sure to the get the kids excited.

One more thing: just between us, you should work on your spelling. And your signature looks like a kid wrote it!

I think this will certainly help Pickens Elementary with the three R's of a great education: reading, writing ... and rides! If you ever think about expanding, let us know. We build great water parks.

Sincerely,

Tim Showtime, manager

Name: _____   Date: _____

Nouns

The Case of Rapunzel's Long Hair

Rapunzel desperately needs to get her hair done for the ball. Can she find someone to help her?

Directions: Underline all the nouns in the letter below. Then go back and circle the proper nouns.

Dear Hair Innovations,

  I need someone to do my hair for the Royal Ball! I've tried everyone else. The hairdresser at Cute Clips fainted when he saw me. The shampoo boys at Fine Styles quit their jobs as soon as I walked in the door. Please, you must help.

  You've probably heard of me. My name is Rapunzel. When I was young, a wicked witch named Wanda kidnapped me and put me in a huge, tall tower. There were no stairs, so she made me grow my hair really long so that she could use it as a ladder. And let me tell you, ever since, my hair has been impossible to manage.

  The witch simply doesn't care how my long, golden locks look. She's very cheap. Doesn't she realize that with 100 feet of hair I need more than just one bottle of Fairytale Shampoo a week? I don't think she expected this extra expense when she put me up in this room.

  I have another problem. My date to the ball, Prince Charming, has been secretly climbing up my hair too. Sometimes he forgets to take off his boots. And even worse, he sometimes doesn't wipe his feet! Gross! Some boys just don't understand women.

  Please say you can help. I need the latest style, and I have to wear my hair up off my shoulders. Otherwise I'm sure King Phillip and the other dancers will get tangled in it. That could be painful.

     Sincerely,
     Rapunzel

Name: _____ Date: _____

The Case of Jack and Jill

Jill wants to explain what really happened when she and Jack went up the hill. But she doesn't understand the difference between *he* and *him*. Can you help her?

Directions: The word *he* or *him* belongs in each of the spaces below. Choose the correct word and write it in.

It was all Jack's fault. I didn't even want to go with

_____ up that hill. Everyone knows that _____

is a troublemaker. _____ is always teasing Mary

about her lamb. But _____ begged me to go with

_____. Frankly, I think _____ has a crush on me.

_____ and I went up the hill. At first we were

having a fine time chatting about basketball, my favorite

sport. It was after the pail was full of water that

_____ and I got into trouble. _____ started

flicking me with water. I asked _____ to stop, but

_____ kept flicking away. _____ is very

immature. I reached over and tried to grab the pail from

_____. _____ got mad and jerked his arm away.

The water spilled all over _____ and me, and we

started to fall. Suddenly, we were both tumbling down the

hill. The pail kept hitting _____ in the head on the

way down. That's why _____ got hurt and I didn't.

Frankly, I would say _____ deserved it!

Grammar Cop's Clues

He and *him* are both personal pronouns. You use both of them as a substitute for someone's name. The key is knowing when to use *he* and when to use *him*. Here are some nifty tricks to help you get it right:

- *He* **is the subject of a sentence or a clause. *He* is used at the beginning of a sentence and right before a verb.** (Example: *He* won the dance contest. When the winner was announced, *he* jumped for joy.)

- *Him* **is the object of a sentence or a clause. *Him* is likely to be at the end of a sentence and after a verb or a preposition.** (Example: Richard called. I told *him* I want to take dancing lessons from *him*.)

Name: _____ Date: _____

Pronouns

The Case of the Old Woman in the Shoe

The Old Woman in the Shoe is thinking about moving to a new home, but she doesn't know the difference between *I* and *me*. Can you help?

Directions: The word *I* or *me* belongs in each of the spaces below. Choose the correct word and write it in.

Do you know _____? _____ am the old

woman who lives in a big shoe. They say I have so many

children, _____ don't know what to do. Actually,

_____ know exactly what to do. I'm selling the shoe

and moving! Do you want to buy a great house? Believe

_____, _____ will make you a good deal.

My children and _____ have been living in

this shoe for years. It was fun at first. When they were

little, they all fit in the heel and _____ could keep

an eye on them. When they got bigger, the girls drove

_____ crazy, swinging on the laces, pretending they

were Tarzan. The boys liked to bodysurf down the tongue

and dive off the toe. Scared _____ to death! And

_____ must say, every year it's a tighter fit.

Next year, _____ will send six of them to

college. As for _____, _____ am thinking

about a simpler life. Maybe I'll move to a little sneaker

in San Francisco. Or a sandal on the beach in Florida.

Between you and _____, this house needs a

little fixing up, but it has a lot of heart and sole!

Grammar Cop's Clues

I **and *me* are both personal pronouns. You use them as a substitute for someone's name. Here are some nifty tricks to help you remember when to use each one:**

- ***I*** **is the subject of a sentence or a clause. *I* is used at the beginning of a sentence and right before a verb.** (Example: *I* like to go to school. In school, *I* hang out with my friends and have fun.)

- ***Me*** **is the object of a sentence or a clause. *Me* is likely to be at the end of a sentence and after a verb or a preposition.** (Example: My friend asked *me* to help him with the homework.)

Pronouns

The Case of a Letter to Old MacDonald

The animals in Old MacDonald's farm are quite upset. So they wrote a letter to Farmer MacDonald. Understandably, they don't know the difference between *we* **and** *us***. Can you help them?**

Directions: In each of the underlined word pairs, circle either *we* or *us*.

Dear Farmer MacDonald,

All these years <u>we/us</u> animals have lived happily on
(1)
your farm, moo-mooing here and cluck-clucking there,

oink-oinking here, and neigh-neighing there. It is <u>we/us</u>
(2)
who have put this farm on the map. <u>We/Us</u> have put your
(3)
song at the top of the nursery school charts. <u>We/Us</u> have
(4)
made you a household name. And what has it gotten

<u>we/us</u>? A big, fat nothing! You have not given <u>we/us</u>
(5)   (6)
animals one dime.

We/Us animals are fed up, Mr. MacDonald. It's
(7)
time for <u>we/us</u> to get our fair share. Do you think <u>we/us</u>
(8)   (9)
animals should go right along mooing and neighing and

oink-oinking and clucking for free? <u>We/Us</u> say, "ee-I-ee-I-No-
(10)
Way!"

Our agent will be contacting you next week.

Sincerely,
Mary O'Mare, the horse
Barb Bovino, the cow
Sid Swine, the pig
Chuck Fowler, the chicken

Grammar Cop's Clues

We and *us* are both personal pronouns. Read these clues to help you know when to use each one:

- *We* **is the subject of a sentence or a clause.** *We* **is used at the beginning of a sentence and right before a verb.** (Example: *We* had a great time at the beach this summer.)

- *Us* **is the object of a sentence or a clause.** *Us* **is likely to be at the end of a sentence and after a verb or a preposition.** (Example: Our mom took *us* out for dinner the other night.)

Plural Nouns

The Case of the Bumbling Cupids

**Big Boss Cupid wrote this memo to America's Cupids.
But he's confused about plurals. Can you help?**

Directions: For each pair of underlined words, circle the
correctly spelled plural noun.

TO: America's Cupids
FROM: Big Boss Cupid

This Valentine's Day, there will be 200

<u>Cupids/Cupides</u> flying around the <u>skys/skies</u>. You will be
   (1)   **(2)**

shooting your <u>arrows/arrowes</u> to bring love and happiness to
                    (3)

lucky <u>couples/couplese</u>.
       (4)

Please be careful. A few years ago, a Cupid (who shall remain nameless) accidentally shot

a walrus, causing her to fall madly in love with Leonardo DiCaprio. These kinds of terrible

<u>mistakes/mistaks</u> give all of us a bad name. Do you know how long it took to get that walrus off
  (5)

the set of *Titanic*?

We must avoid these <u>disasters/disasteres</u> in the future. Here are some <u>tipps/tips</u> to help you.
                         (6)   **(7)**

    1. Practice your <u>landings/landinges</u>. Avoid slippery <u>rooves/roofs</u>. No one likes to see a
                         (8)   **(9)**

      naked Cupid falling into <u>bushes/bushs</u> or <u>mailboxs/mailboxes</u>.
                            (10)   **(11)**

    2. Sharpen the <u>points/pointes</u> of your arrows. A dull arrow is likely to bounce right off
                  (12)

      your target.

    3. Wear your <u>glasses/glassess</u>. If you can't see clearly, how can you be sure you're
                (13)

      shooting the right person? Glasses also protect you from getting <u>flys/flies</u> in your
                                                            (14)

      <u>eyes/eyies</u>.
      (15)

These simple rules will help make this the best holiday ever!

Name: _____ Date: _____

The Apology of Goldilocks

Goldilocks feels guilty about messing up the home of the three bears. She wants to make it up to them. But she doesn't understand the laws of possessive words. Can you help her?

Directions: Wherever you see a blank line, decide whether the word needs an *'s*, an *s'* or a plain *s*. Write your answer on the blank.

Dear Mama Bear, Papa Bear, and Baby Bear,

I owe you guy__ an apology. I didn't mean to get my germ__ all over everyone__ porridge and break Baby Bear__ chair. I didn't say to myself, "I think I'll head to the bear__ cottage and mess up their stuff." I had been hiking through the wood__, gathering rock__ for my science project. I had stuffed all the rocks into my jumper__ pocket. When I sat down in Baby Bear__ chair, the rock__ weight caused me to crush the chair.

To make it up to you, I would like you to come to my family__ house for dinner. I have a new chair for Baby Bear. (I used all my baby-sitting money to pay for it.) Please let me know if you can come.

Love,

Goldilocks

P.S. I'll be serving some of my parent__ homemade honey.

Grammar Cop's Clues

Remember these basic laws of possessives and plurals:

- **Singular possessive ('s): Use 's when you want to show that something belongs to someone or something.** (Example: That is *Bozo's* clown wig.)

- **Plural possessive (s'): Use s' when something belongs to more than one person.** (Example: Those are the *clowns'* wigs.)

- **Plural noun (s): Use a plain s when you simply want to show that there is more than one of something.** (Example: There are lots of *clowns* in town. They are all wearing *wigs*.)

Verbs

The Case of Mary Had a Little Rooster

It seems that Mary didn't just have a little lamb. She had a rooster as well. And he's mad! He wants to tell us why he's so angry, but he doesn't know how to use verbs correctly. Can you help him?

Directions: Circle the correct verb from each underlined pair.

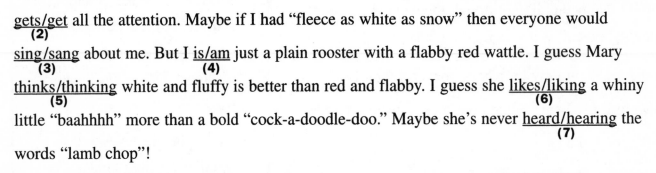

Mary had a little rooster
With a very clever mind.
And everywhere that Mary went
The rooster was left behind.

I bet you've never <u>heard/hearing</u> that verse
(1)
before. Do you know why? It's because that silly lamb

<u>gets/get</u> all the attention. Maybe if I had "fleece as white as snow" then everyone would
(2)

<u>sing/sang</u> about me. But I <u>is/am</u> just a plain rooster with a flabby red wattle. I guess Mary
(3)   (4)

<u>thinks/thinking</u> white and fluffy is better than red and flabby. I guess she <u>likes/liking</u> a whiny
(5)   (6)

little "baahhhh" more than a bold "cock-a-doodle-doo." Maybe she's never <u>heard/hearing</u> the
(7)

words "lamb chop"!

You think I didn't <u>try/tried</u> to follow her to school one day? I <u>tried/try</u> all right. And you
(8)   (9)

know what that little lamb <u>do/did</u>? He tripped me so I <u>fell/fall</u> down the hill that gave Jack and
(10)   (11)

Jill their problems. By the time I got to school, that lamb was there. He got <u>sent/send</u> to the
(12)

principal's office. I bet they were afraid that lamb would <u>give/giving</u> everyone lice.
(13)

I've never <u>hearing/heard</u> of a rooster with lice, have you? Why doesn't anyone
(14)

<u>write/writing</u> a song about that?
(15)

Verbs

The Case of the Dog Who Eats Homework

Molly the Mutt has something shocking to tell, but she doesn't know which verbs to use. Can you help?

Directions: For each pair of underlined words, circle the correct verb.

From the Desk of Molly the Mutt

Dear Teachers,

The first thing I <u>want / wants</u> to say is that
                        (1)
I'm sorry. Sort of.

Let me explain. I'm sure there are times

when a student <u>come / comes</u> to class without his or
                    (2)
her homework. You patiently <u>ask / asks</u> where it is, and your
                                (3)
student <u>reply / replies</u>, "The dog ate it!" You tend to think that your student <u>has / have</u> a big
        (4)   **(5)**
imagination and is just making up a story. Well, it's all my fault. I <u>confess / confessing</u>.
                                                                        (6)

I, Molly the Mutt, <u>eat / eats</u> homework. And lots of it. I <u>travel / traveling</u> from state to
                    (7)   **(8)**
state, house to house, devouring homework.

I'm not picky. I'll eat anything I can <u>get / gets</u> my paws on. I <u>like / likes</u> essays,
                                        (9)   **(10)**
vocabulary lists, even math workbooks. Dog food <u>is / are</u> just not interesting to me anymore.
                                                  (11)
There is nothing better than a hearty meal of note cards from a 4th-grade oral report on George

Washington. Though I'd have to say my most favorite treat <u>was / were</u> Karl Butler's book report
                                                            (12)
on *Green Eggs and Ham*. That was so tasty, so delicious!

So the next time your student <u>show / shows</u> up in class with a scrap of torn notebook
                                (13)
paper covered in slobber, I'm responsible.

Catch me if you can!

Sincerely,

Molly the Mutt

P.S. I even started to eat this letter after I <u>typed / typing</u> it!
                                                (14)

Verbs

The Case of the Cat Food Casserole

Would you feed your family cat-food casserole? Not on purpose, maybe. Read this confession from a budding chef.

Directions: On each blank line, write the past tense form of the verb that appears below it. We did the first one for you.

I think that last night my family _ate_ cat food
(eat)

for dinner. And, I think it was my fault. Here's what

_____:
(happen)

My dad was making tuna casserole. He had already _____ the celery,
(slice)

_____ the onion, and _____ the noodles when the phone _____.
(chop)   (cook)   (ring)

I _____ that I would finish making dinner while he _____ on the phone.
(whisper)   (talk)

I had, after all, _____ my parents make tuna casserole hundreds of times. "Just leave it to
(watch)

me," I _____.
(say)

I _____ a can of tuna from the cupboard above the sink and _____ its
(grab)   (dump)

contents into a casserole dish along with everything else. Then I _____ it all together and
(mix)

_____ it in the oven. My family _____ the casserole, and I _____
(stick)   (love)   (feel)

very proud of myself!

I _____ still feeling proud this morning when my mom _____ me to
(am)   (ask)

feed our cat, Benjamin. "There's one can of cat food left. It's in the cupboard above the sink," she

said. But when I _____ the cupboard, I _____ not see any cat food. All I
(open)   (do)

_____ was one can of tuna fish. One can of tuna fish that _____ exactly the
(see)   (is)

same shape and size as the can I had _____ into last night's casserole....
(empty)

So, do I tell them that they _____ cat food? It's not like the cat food
(eat)

_____ them in any way. I think it might be better for everyone if I keep the truth to
(hurt)

myself. Or maybe I'll share it with Benjamin, as I feed him the leftover casserole.

Name: _____ Date: _____

Adjectives/Adverbs

The Case of the Saxophone Disaster

Oops! Marcia's big mistake got her kicked out of the school band. But was it really her fault? You decide.

Directions: Circle all the adjectives and underline all the adverbs in the letter below.

Dear Mom and Dad,

   I have a little problem. Mr. Willis suddenly kicked me out of the band. He called me a troublemaker. But it's all a big mistake! Here's the whole story:

   Remember last Friday when you told me to thoroughly clean my closet? Well, what I didn't tell you is that while I was cleaning, I lost dear Zippy. I took her out of her cozy tank so she could keep me company. But I must have lost her in my closet. You have repeatedly told me my closet is ridiculously messy. And you're right. You wouldn't believe the crazy stuff I found in there! Do you remember that pepperoni pizza we couldn't find? And Dad, are you missing some fuzzy, purple slippers?

   Anyway, I never found poor Zippy. I figured she was slithering happily in the closet. I thought I would find her eventually. Snakes like pepperoni pizza, right?

   So I went to the recital. We started playing "Oops … I Did It Again." Suddenly the girl next to me screamed loudly. Zippy was sticking her little, green head out of my saxophone! I swear she was dancing. The rest of the band was not charmed, and they quickly ran off the stage. Mr. Willis closed the front curtain. He angrily told me I was fired from the band!

   Do you think Mr. Willis will forgive me? And what about Zippy? That snake's got some serious groove! Do you think she can audition for the next *American Idol*?

                    Your sorry daughter,
                    Marcia

Grammar Cop's Clues

Remember these simple rules about adjectives and adverbs:

- An *adjective* describes a noun or a pronoun. It might tell what kind, which one, or how many. (Example: Mr. Bean bought those *delicious red* apples for us.)

- An *adverb* describes a verb, an adjective, or another adverb. Many adverbs end in *-ly*. (Example: We tiptoed *quietly* past the sleeping dog.)

Name: _____ Date: _____

Adjectives/Adverbs

The Case of the Unexpected Delay

Will the Gingerbread Man's delicious new house ever be completed? Not if the hungry workers can help it!

Directions: Circle all the adjectives and underline all the adverbs in the letter below.

Dear Mr. Gingerbread Man,

We have some bad news. The big additions you asked us to build on your gingerbread house haven't been going as originally planned. Something strange is happening. Please let me humbly explain.

You must know that coconut lollipops, sticky Snickers® bars, and giant candy canes are not normal materials for building a new bedroom. But when I asked my loyal employees, they said that they would joyfully welcome the unusual challenge. Big Tony was especially excited. He even started anxiously licking his lips.

On the first day of work, I noticed that we were using up purple gumdrops faster than I'd expected. And the order I had placed for giant jawbreakers was short by nearly a hundred. Then the huge crate of red licorice we were using for the inside walls disappeared!

Suddenly my favorite workers are regularly calling in sick. Heavy Hank told me he had seventeen cavities. He's going to be out for a week getting them professionally drilled. Chubby Chuck has gotten so chubby that he fell through the graham-cracker roof. I don't know what's happening to them. Maybe they need more physical exercise.

Please, just give us more time. We'll quickly do a wonderful job.

Sincerely,
Do-It-All Builders, Inc.

Grammar Cop's Clues

Remember these simple rules about adjectives and adverbs:

- **An *adjective* describes a noun or a pronoun. It might tell what kind, which one, or how many.** (Example: My *two* best friends gave me the most *wonderful* surprise ever!)

- **An *adverb* describes a verb, an adjective, or another adverb. Many adverbs end in *-ly*.** (Example: I *quickly* finished my homework so I could watch TV.)

Name: _____ Date: _____

the case of the missing capital letters

The person who wrote this letter didn't really understand the laws of capital letters. Can you help find the mistakes?

Directions: Circle the letters that should have been capitalized. (Hint: There are 20 mistakes.)

Dear cinderella and Prince Charming,

there must be a terrible mistake! the stepsisters and I have not yet received an invitation to your wedding. i keep telling the stepsisters that the invitation will arrive soon. i'm getting worried that our invitation got lost. i hear you often have problems with the unicorns that deliver the palace mail.

I'm sure you intend to invite us! After all, you were always my special favorite. How i spoiled you! i let you do all the best chores around the house. are you still mad about that trip to disney world? i don't know how we could have forgotten you! anyway, florida is too hot in the summer.

so cinderella dear, please send along another invitation as soon as you can. i know how busy you are in your new palace! if you need any cleaning help, i can send one of your stepsisters along. they both miss you so much!

Best wishes,
Your Not-Really-So-Wicked Stepmother

Grammar Cop's Clues

Remember these basic laws of capital letters:

- **Names: Always capitalize someone's proper name.** (Example: Gina, Kenneth, Terrence)

- **Places: Always capitalize the name of a town, city, state, or country.** (Example: I live in Orchard Beach, California, which is in the United States.)

- **I: Always capitalize the letter *I* when it stands for a person.** (Example: I am in fourth grade and I'm 10 years old.)

- **First letter: Always capitalize the first letter of a sentence.**

Capitalization

The Case of the Fairy Godmother for Hire

Belinda Cunningham is looking for a job. She wrote this business letter, but she is confused about the use of capital letters. Can you help her?

Directions: Circle the letters that should be capitalized. Draw a line through the capital letters that should be lowercase. (Hint: There are 19 mistakes.)

mollie O'Brien
4485 Problem street
New york, NY 10009

February 28, 2004

dear Ms. O'Brien,

      I am writing in response to The classified ad that appeared in *Magic Wand Weekly* ("fairy godmother wanted"). my many years of experience make Me highly qualified for this position.

      You may already be familiar with my work. One of my former clients, Cinderella, received quite a bit of attention. With my help, She married Prince luckyfellow and moved into that castle (the real one looks nothing like that tacky thing at disney world). Of course, I would want to work with you to determine the happy ending that's right for you, were i to become your fairy godmother.

      I currently live in palm Beach, florida. There, i keep quite busy, thank you. My book, *Turning vegetables into Vehicles,* has been on the best-seller list since last april. I am also developing my own line of glass footwear.

      If you want to speak to my former clients, feel free to contact Cinderella, Sleeping beauty, and Michael Jordan (talent only goes so far, my dear).

      If you would like to meet me, just close your eyes and make a wish. I will appear immediately.

                 sincerely,
                 Belinda Cunningham

Grammar Cop's Clues

Remember these basic laws of capital letters:

- **Names: Always capitalize someone's proper name.** (Example: Gina, Kenneth, Terrence)

- **Places: Always capitalize the name of a town, city, state, or country.** (Example: I live in Orchard Beach, California, which is in the United States.)

- **I: Always capitalize the letter *I* when it stands for a person.** (Example: I am in fourth grade and I'm 10 years old.)

- **First letter: Always capitalize the first letter of a sentence.**

Name: _____   Date: _____

Capitalization

The Case of Freddy's Tarantula

Freddy may never get his dream pet, but maybe he can teach his mom and dad some rules about capitalizing family titles. Can you?

Directions: In the letter below, all of the family titles (like mom and uncle) have been underlined. Circle the ones that should begin with a capital letter.

TO: Freddy

FROM: <u>mom</u> and <u>dad</u>
             (1)   **(2)**

SUBJECT: Your birthday present request

Dear Freddy,

     Your <u>mom</u> and I read with great interest your birthday
(3)
wish list. You know <u>mom</u> and I love you. We want your tenth
(4)
birthday to be a huge hit. Your <u>grandfather</u> already picked up
(5)
the bowling shoes, and <u>aunt</u> Marjorie wants to get you the
(6)
glow-in-the-dark socks. However, we're having a little trouble
with item number three on your list: the tarantula.

     You know <u>mom</u> and I are glad you love animals. But
(7)
really, Freddy, do you think a tarantula is a good pet for a
10-year-old? How would your <u>grandparents</u> react? I don't
(8)
think saying, "<u>grandma</u>, meet the newest addition to the
(9)
Horowitz family" will work. Your sweet <u>granny</u> would run
(10)
screaming from the house. And forget about your <u>uncle</u>.
(11)
Don't you know that <u>uncle</u> Clayton is terrified of spiders?
(12)
     To be honest, <u>mom</u> and I don't feel that a venomous
(13)
spider fits our idea of a cuddly household pet. If you want
something small and furry, your <u>mother</u> and I will buy you a
                                  (14)
couple of hamsters.

             Much love,

             <u>dad</u>
             (15)

Grammar Cop's Clues

How do you know whether to capitalize family titles like *mom*, *grandma*, and *uncle*? Here are some tricks:

- **If you're using the word as part of a person's name (Aunt Rhoda) or as a substitute for a person's name ("Did Grandma call?"), capitalize it. You are using it as a proper noun.**

- **Otherwise, do not capitalize it; you are not using it as a proper noun. Here's a hint: When you use a word like *my*, *your*, or *her* before the family title ("My mom has red hair"), you usually do not capitalize the title.**

Capitalization

The Case of Frosty's Rules

It seems that some of the snowpeople need to be reminded of the rules of the trade. Too bad Frosty can't seem to remember the rules of capitalization. Can you help him?

Directions: Circle the letters that should be capitalized.

dear fellow snowmen and snowwomen,

it's that time of year again, when fall turns to winter and the snowy season approaches. to make sure this will be a great season for all of us, i want to remind you of a few important rules:

1. **don't eat your face.** i know you get hungry out there. no matter what, though, do not eat your carrot nose and raisin eyes. have a little self-respect.
2. **do not peek in windows.** i don't care if the minnesota vikings are playing the buffalo bills. no human wants to discover a snowperson peeking through the window. last year, julius iceman was nabbed by the minneapolis police department watching *how the grinch stole christmas* through the melville family's window. he melted in the backseat of the squad car.
3. **do not play gameboy.** do i need to remind you that video games will turn your brain to slush? there are plenty of other ways to entertain yourself out there in the yard.

   i know this will be a fantastic season. if you have any questions, call me at my pre-season headquarters, the freezer section of stop & shop.

sincerely,
frosty

Grammar Cop's Clues

Remember these basic laws of capital letters:

- **Names: Always capitalize someone's proper name.** (For example: Gina, Kenneth, Terrence)

- **Places: Always capitalize the name of a town, city, state, or country.** (Example: I live in Orchard Beach, California, which is in the United States.)

- **I: Always capitalize the letter *I* when it stands for a person.** (Example: I am in fourth grade and I'm 10 years old.)

- **First letter: Always capitalize the first letter of a sentence.**

Name: _____ Date: _____

Contractions

The Case of Humpty Dumpty

Humpty Dumpty has written a letter to all the king's horses and all the king's men, but he doesn't know how to make contractions. Can you help?

Directions: A *contraction* is formed by putting together two words with certain letters left out. An *apostrophe* (') takes the place of the missing letters. For each underlined, numbered word pair, write the correct contraction in the blanks on the right. We did the first one for you.

Dear All the King's Horses and All the King's Men,

     HELP! Have you forgotten that <u>I am</u> still lying here next to
                      (1)

the wall? I <u>do not</u> mean to be a pest. <u>You are</u> all very busy with
    (2)   **(3)**

your royal responsibilities. But you <u>should not</u> have just left me
                                (4)

here! <u>Do not</u> you think you could have tried a little harder to put
     (5)

me back together again? My feet <u>are not</u> even attached to my legs.
                     (6)

I <u>cannot</u> find one of my ears. And I <u>do not</u> know what became of
  (7)   **(8)**

my top hat. <u>I am</u> worried that one of Cinderella's stepsisters took it.
       (9)

     The situation <u>could not</u> be more dangerous. You know that
               (10)

diner across the street? <u>It is</u> only a matter of time before I show up
            (11)

on its menu: *Humpty Dumpty over easy with bacon and home*

fries.

     <u>I will</u> give a big hug to the person who gets me back on my
   (12)

feet. Hurry!

                     Sincerely,

                     Mr. Humpty Dumpty

1.   I'm
2. _____
3. _____
4. _____
5. _____
6. _____
7. _____
8. _____
9. _____
10. _____
11. _____
12. _____

Name: _____ **Date:** _____

Contractions

The Case of the Grumpy Goose

This goose is fed up and confused—confused about the use of contractions. Can you help her?

Directions: A *contraction* is formed by putting together two words with certain letters left out. An *apostrophe* (') takes the place of the missing letters. For each underlined, numbered word pair, write the correct contraction in the blanks on the right. We did the first one for you.

<u>You are</u> probably aware that the game
(1)

"Duck, Duck, Goose" <u>does not</u> require the participation of an actual
(2)

goose. Well, some of the people around here seem to have forgotten

that. Lately, no matter where I am, <u>somebody is</u> after me. I <u>cannot</u>
(3) **(4)**

explain it, but <u>it is</u> driving me crazy!
(5)

    For example, the other day I was resting behind the barn.

<u>I had</u> just finished a delicious crust of bread and <u>could not</u> have been
(6) **(7)**

feeling more relaxed. Suddenly, the farmer's boy came by and

whacked me on the head.

    "Goose!" he yelled and started chasing me around the pond.

"I <u>do not</u> want to play this game!" I screamed as I ran. "Plus,
(8)

<u>you are</u> playing it wrong. I'm supposed to chase you!" But he
(9)

<u>would not</u> listen. He caught me and demanded that I sit in the
(10)

mushpot (whatever that is).

    Please help me. <u>I will</u> try anything to end this foolishness. We
(11)

geese <u>are not</u> safe anymore. The best <u>I have</u> been able to do so far is
(12) **(13)**

buy a good pair of running shoes!

1. You're
2. _____
3. _____
4. _____
5. _____
6. _____
7. _____
8. _____
9. _____
10. _____
11. _____
12. _____
13. _____

Name: _____ Date: _____

Contractions

The Case of the Sick Bookworm

Neither Mr. Worm nor Dr. Fish understands the use of contractions. Can you help them?

Directions: A *contraction* is formed by putting together two words with certain letters left out. An *apostrophe* (') takes the place of the missing letters. For each of the underlined, numbered word pairs, write the correct contraction in the blanks on the right. We did the first one for you.

Dear Dr. Fish,

     I hope <u>you will</u> be able to help me. <u>I am</u> the bookworm who
           (1)   **(2)**
lives in the New York Public Library. Ever since gulping down

Meet the Backstreet Boys last week, <u>I have</u> been suffering from a
                                  (3)
mysterious stomach illness. Normally, I can munch through

Shakespeare's complete plays and still have room for a chapter

from *Treasure Island*. Now, I can barely make it through *Romeo*

and Juliet! Also, <u>I had</u> been nibbling on a chapter from *Little*
           (4)
House on the Prairie when suddenly I <u>could not</u> stop belching up
                              (5)
adjectives. It happened again with *The Hobbit*. Not only is this

problem embarrassing, but if the librarian hears me, <u>she will</u> be
                                      (6)
furious. Help me! I <u>cannot</u> eat my favorite books!
               (7)

• •

Dear Mr. Worm,

     First, <u>you are</u> eating too many big words. You must
           (8)
immediately begin a strict diet of three-letter words. I prescribe

Dr. Seuss's *Hop on Pop*. After that, try a few pages of *Goodnight*

Moon, but avoid all words with more than two syllables! As for

your mysterious stomach illness, well, I <u>do not</u> think <u>it is</u> very
                                 (9)   **(10)**
mysterious at all! The answer is obvious: no more *Meet the*

Backstreet Boys. It clearly <u>does not</u> agree with you. Stick to this
                           (11)
diet for a few weeks and <u>you will</u> be back to your luscious
                     (12)
Shakespeare in no time.

1.   you'll
2. _____
3. _____
4. _____
5. _____
6. _____
7. _____
8. _____
9. _____
10. _____
11. _____
12. _____

Name: _____   **Date:** _____

Contractions

The Case of the Chicken That Crossed the Road

This chicken has something to say. Can you give him some help with contractions?

Directions: A *contraction* is formed by putting together two words with certain letters left out. An *apostrophe* (') takes the place of the missing letters. For each of the underlined, numbered word pairs, write the correct contraction in the blanks on the right. We did the first one for you.

"Why did the chicken cross the road?"

<u>You have</u> heard this joke, <u>have not</u> you? <u>You are</u> laughing
  (1)   **(2)**   **(3)**
right now, just thinking about it, <u>are not</u> you? Well, <u>I am</u> the chicken
                            (4)   **(5)**
who crossed the road, and <u>I will</u> tell you something. I <u>do not</u> find
                    (6)   **(7)**
that joke funny at all.

Since the day I was hatched, <u>I have</u> minded my own business.
                          (8)
<u>It is</u> not like me to cause trouble or draw attention to myself. And
(9)
yet, <u>you have</u> turned me into a big joke. <u>Is not</u> it time to end this
   (10)   **(11)**
mockery?

So <u>here is</u> what really happened: <u>I had</u> spent the morning with
  (12)   **(13)**
my friends—a real cluckfest. <u>We had</u> had a few laughs, and quite a
                      (14)
few cans of soda. On the way home, I had to go to the bathroom.

I looked across the road, and there was a gas station with a nice

clean restroom. So I did it. I crossed the road. I used the restroom

and went on my way. <u>That is</u> the whole story.
                    (15)

So the next time someone asks you why the chicken crossed

the road, you <u>will not</u> giggle, chuckle, or snort. <u>You will</u> tell him the
          (16)   **(17)**
truth: "When a chicken's gotta go, a chicken's gotta go."

1. _You've_
2. _____
3. _____
4. _____
5. _____
6. _____
7. _____
8. _____
9. _____
10. _____
11. _____
12. _____
13. _____
14. _____
15. _____
16. _____
17. _____

Punctuation

The Case of the Wanna-be Superstar

This budding superstar is trying to convince his parents to support his ambitions. Too bad he doesn't know the first thing about punctuation. Can you help him?

Directions: Fill in the correct punctuation marks in the letter below.

Dear Mom and Dad

I'm going to be a star I saw an ad for Starmakers in the back of a comic book For two years they have made their name by turning youngsters like me into pop music idols—overnight I just need $1,000 for their how-to book Can I have a loan

If I'm going to become a superstar I'll need a new hairstyle A neon green mohawk will look great on stage Also you'll need to buy a limousine I can't bear having you pick me up from school in the minivan anymore It doesn't fit my new image I just know crowds will come every night to hear me sing I have real talent After all these years of listening to me in the shower you must know that I'm great Even Bubba loves howling along to my version of "The Star-Spangled Banner"

I'll sell millions of records You'll see my picture in hundreds of magazines This could be my big break So can I have the $1,000 Of course I'll pay you back when I become a multi-millionaire I'll save every cent honest Please don't say no Do you think the principal would excuse me from school for a world tour with Avril

Your son
Billy

Punctuation

The Case of the Weary Lunch Lady

If this letter from the students at Webster Elementary doesn't convince the lunch lady to change the lunch menu, then nothing will. Too bad these kids don't know how to use punctuation marks. Can you help?

Directions: Fill in the correct punctuation marks in the letter below.

Dear Lunch Lady Ruth

      Lately we students have noticed that you seem overworked You look tired Your hairnet is always on crooked You can barely keep your eyes open as we slide our trays by you Once you dumped a ladleful of gravy on Tommy's head His mom was not pleased when she got the dry-cleaning bill for his Boy Scout uniform

      It can't be easy to feed all of us It must take hours of chopping broccoli slicing brussels sprouts and cooking lima beans to fix lunch for hundreds of students Things need to change Don't get us wrong We appreciated the liver meatballs you fixed for us last Thursday Just because that food fight started before we could eat any of them doesn't mean we wouldn't have loved the meal Those meatballs were just so easy to throw They bounced nicely too Oh and sorry you had to clean up the cafeteria afterwards Still it was pretty impressive how high we got those spaghetti noodles stuck up on the wall wasn't it

      Let us make a suggestion Candy corn and jelly beans require absolutely no preparation in the kitchen Just grab a bunch set them on the plate and hand them to us hungry students We'll be happy to put them in our stomachs not on each other Can Swedish Fish provide us with protein Candy Corn is a vegetable right

      We hope you will consider our proposal

                            Sincerely

                            The Students of Webster Elementary

Name: _____   Date: _____

Quotation Marks

The Three Little Pigs' Day in Court

The Three Little Pigs are trying to prove their case against the Big Bad Wolf. But they don't know the rules for using quotation marks. Can you help by adding the quotation marks needed in their story?

Directions: Insert quotation marks in the correct places below.

One day the Three Little Pigs—Hambone, Porky, and Daisy—agreed that Wolf had bothered them long enough. I hate to be a pig, Daisy said, but I think we should sue him.

A few weeks later, they went to court. The courtroom was packed with other animals.

What's the problem? asked the judge.

Wolf won't leave us alone, said Hambone. He keeps blowing down our houses.

Porky said, He turned my house into a pigsty! The judge asked Wolf if the charges were true. They're all hogwash, said Wolf. I'm not guilty.

The judge said that he didn't know what to believe. Do you have witnesses? he asked the pigs.

The pigs looked to the other animals for help, but they all said that they were scared of Wolf.

The pigs were losing hope when a flea jumped out of Wolf's fur. I saw everything, she said. The pigs are telling the truth. Wolf is a real beast!

What a relief, Daisy said. Maybe now we'll all live happily ever after!

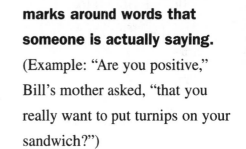

Grammar Cop's Clues

Remember these basic laws for quotation marks:

- **Direct Quotes: Put quotation marks around words that someone is actually saying.** (Example: "Are you positive," Bill's mother asked, "that you really want to put turnips on your sandwich?")

- **Indirect Quotes: Don't put quotation marks around words that summarize what someone said.** (Example: Bill said that he likes to eat turnips at every meal.)
  Tip: Phrases such as *said that* or *reported that* are often good clues that you don't need quotation marks.

Name: _____ Date: _____

The Case of the Frog Prince

Ever since Prince Leonardo was turned into a frog, his spelling skills have really suffered. His letter below is filled with spelling errors. Can you help him?

Directions: Circle each misspelled word. Then write down the correct spelling in the spaces provided below. Hint: There are 20 misspelled words.

Dear Madam Witch,

     I am writting to you to tell you how dissapointed I am that you have refussed to tern me back into a prince. I have apoligized over and over agian for making that little coment about the wart on your nose. I have suffered enougf! If you don't think so, turn yourself into a frog and see what it is like. I must share my pond with three verry nasty geese. The pond water is recking my skin. And the food is terible (altho I did catch a most delishous fly yesterday for lunch). I miss my palase!

     In your last letter, you told me that the spell will be broken when a princess gives me a kiss. I am afrade that there is a real shortage of princesses around the kingdom. Most are off at collige. If a princess did happen to see me at the pond, I somehow dout she would want to kiss me.

     Please, won't you reconsidder? You know wear to find me: on the second rock to the rite.

              Best wishes,

              Prince Leonardo

              (the geese call me Prince Slimo)

P.S. If you turn me back into a prince, I'll pay the finest doctor to take care of that little problem in your nasal area.

1. _____
2. _____
3. _____
4. _____
5. _____
6. _____
7. _____
8. _____
9. _____
10. _____
11. _____
12. _____
13. _____
14. _____
15. _____
16. _____
17. _____
18. _____
19. _____
20. _____

Name: _____ Date: _____

Spelling

The Case of the Careless Typist

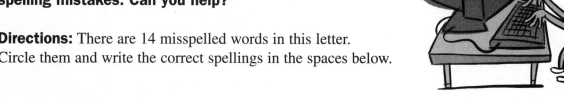

Author Johanna Hurwitz has written a letter to all the *Storyworks* **readers, but whoever typed it made some spelling mistakes. Can you help?**

Directions: There are 14 misspelled words in this letter. Circle them and write the correct spellings in the spaces below.

Dear *Storyworks* Readers,

What fun I've had reeding the entries to the "Create a Character" contest. In fact, in the end, it even inspired me to right a story about a contest.

Grand Prize winner Mika Roy may wonder why I didn't include many peices of information about Juniper Green. This is because authors always know lots more about there characters than they tell in their stories. By knowing details such as faverite foods, TV programs, and hobbies, and even the dislikes of my characters, I understan them better and am better able to write about them.

One thing that fassinated me was that so many of you who entered this contest wrote about a character who lived in a town diferent from your own. I think this is because young writers always think things are more inneresting elsewhere. When I was your age, the stories I wrote all took place in faraway places wear I'd never been. My addvice to you is to write about your own community. You know it better and if you think for a while, you'll descover that there are many things that you can write about.

Congratulations to all who entered. You all did a great job!

Your friend,
Johanna

P.S. Here's a secrit from my past: I entered some writing contests when I was your age and I never won. I geuss my writing improved as I got older.

1. _____

2. _____

3. _____

4. _____

5. _____

6. _____

7. _____

8. _____

9. _____

10. _____

11. _____

12. _____

13. _____

14. _____

Name: _____ Date: _____

The Case of the Terrible Tooth Fairy

There are problems in Tooth Fairy Land. This letter will be sent to the queen, but it's filled with spelling mistakes! Can you help?

Directions: Circle the misspelled words in the letter below. Write them correctly in the blanks on the right. Hint: There are 15 misspelled words.

TO: Queen Tooth Fairy
FROM: Complaint Bureau

Over the past month, I have recieved five complaints about tooth fairy number 324, also known as Doris. Last Friday, on a job in Montana, she stopped in the kichen and made herself a lettuce and wipped cream sandwish. She left a big mess. Then, she took a nap in the kid's doll house.

Afterwords, she turned on a Backstreet Boys CD and started dansing on the bed. The little girl woke up and started screeming. The mother thought Doris was a giant mosquito and went after her with a can of bug spray. Doris escaped, but we nearley had a disaster. I don't have to tell you what would happen if the newspapers herd about this.

As you know, all tooth fairies are trained at the Tooth Fairy Command Center. The rules are clear. They are to fly into a room quietley and carfully inspect the tooth under the pillow, without waking up the child. If they beleive the tooth is real (fake teeth are a growing probblem) they are to leave fifty cents. They are then to exit the house without making any noise.

Doris is a hopeless case. I believe you should help her find a job with anuther organization. I undorstand the Easter Bunny needs some help this year.

1. _____

2. _____

3. _____

4. _____

5. _____

6. _____

7. _____

8. _____

9. _____

10. _____

11. _____

12. _____

13. _____

14. _____

15. _____

Name: _____   Date: _____

Spelling

The Case of the Missing Rabbit

The class rabbit has disappeared, and now there's a wild bunny on the loose. Could they be the same animal?

Directions: Decide whether each of the numbered "*ie*" and "*ei*" words is spelled correctly. Circle the ones that are spelled incorrectly. Hint: There are 8 mistakes.

Dear Mrs. Washington,

   As you know, I <u>received</u> permission to take
   (1)

care of our class rabbit, Binky, over summer

vacation. I fed him a <u>vareity</u> of vegetables every day. I changed his water and cleaned his cage,
   (2)

but something went wrong. A few weeks ago, he disappeared. I hung "missing bunny" posters all

over the <u>neighborhood</u>, but nobody had seen him. Then, things started getting <u>wierd</u>.
   (3)   (4)

   First, I found a copy of the book *The Runaway Bunny* hidden in his cage. Then, I read that

the Stop & Shop had been robbed. <u>Eight</u> bags of carrots, a head of lettuce, and a pair of pink
   (5)

sunglasses were stolen. A <u>casheir</u> reported that she saw a gang of rabbits hopping away from the
   (6)

store. She claimed <u>thier</u> leader was a large rabbit with black and white spots. He was wearing the
   (7)

sunglasses.

   At first, I didn't <u>beleive</u> it. <u>Niether</u> did my friends. But, Mrs. Washington, I think we all
   (8)   (9)

know who that large rabbit was. I think Binky was the mastermind of the grocery store <u>heist</u>.
   (10)

   I hope you don't blame me for the fact that our class rabbit has turned out to be a <u>theif</u>.
   (11)

I don't know what happened—he was always so <u>quiet</u> and sweet! Maybe, if he goes to jail, we
   (12)

could take a <u>feild</u> trip to visit him. Anyway, I think our next class pet should be a goldfish.
   (13)

   Sincerely,

   Joseph

Name: _____   Date: _____

Homophones

The Case of Frosty the Snowman

Frosty the Snowman has a complaint, but he is confused about homophones. Can you help?

Directions: *Homophones* are words that sound the same but have different spellings and different meanings. Circle the correct word in each pair of underlined words below.

From the Desk of Frosty the Snowman

I <u>know/no</u> you all think that I am a "jolly,
(1)

happy <u>soul/sole</u>." That's really not the case. I
(2)

mean, my eyes are made out of coal. I can't <u>sea/see</u> a thing! That's why I am always going
(3)

"thumpety-thump-thump" all over town.

Everyone thinks I came alive only because those kids put a silk hat on my head. I was

already alive, but I was just freezing cold. I'm <u>maid/made</u> of snow, after all! Do you <u>know/no</u> that
(4)   (5)

most of your body heat escapes <u>through/threw</u> the top of your head? That's why it's important to
(6)

<u>where/wear</u> a hat in the winter.
(7)

Please, don't even get me started on my <u>knows/nose</u>! It doesn't work at all. First it was a
(8)

button, now it's a carrot. Everybody is always roasting chestnuts, and I have absolutely no

<u>sense/cents</u> of smell. Plus, my nose barely stays on my face. I sneezed once and that thing
(9)

<u>flue/flew</u> right off. It took me an <u>hour/our</u> to find it.
(10)   (11)

And do you <u>know/no</u> why I was running here and <u>their/there</u> all over the square? Because
(12)   (13)

those kids were chasing me! They even <u>through/threw</u> snowballs at me! I had to use my
(14)

broomstick as a shield.

Oh well, at least it's not July.

Name: _____ Date: _____

Homophones

The Case of the Cow Who Jumped Over the Moon

Hey diddle, diddle, does anyone know what happened to the cow who jumped over the moon? Well, we finally found out. In this exclusive letter to *Storyworks*, the cow tells us about her new life.

Directions: *Homophones* are words that sound the same but have different spellings and different meanings. For each pair of underlined homophones, circle the correct word.

Greetings, Earthlings!

We all <u>know/no</u> that the dish ran away with
    (1)
the spoon, and they lived happily ever after (for six months). I bet you are all dying to know what

happened to me after my famous jump over the moon. Now that I have my very own

<u>stationary/stationery</u>, I decided to <u>right/write</u> to you. Yes, I jumped over the moon, but I did not
    (2)   **(3)**

land back on Earth. I kept flying <u>through/threw</u> the night sky all the <u>way/weigh</u> to the planet
                 (4)   **(5)**

Venus. At first I didn't know <u>wear/where</u> I was. It turns out I'm not the only <u>won/one</u> who lives
          (6)   **(7)**

on Venus. One of the three <u>bears/bares</u> built a house here. I <u>see/sea</u> Little Red Riding Hood
        (8)   **(9)**

skipping around. We are all very happy and we <u>meet/meat</u> once a <u>week/weak</u> for our book club.
         (10)   **(11)**

Life <u>here/hear</u> on Venus is a little bit strange. Let me try <u>to/too</u> explain. It takes longer for
    (12)   **(13)**

Venus to rotate once than it does for it to orbit the <u>son/sun</u>. That means that on Venus, a day is
        (14)

longer than a year! I know, I know, it's confusing. And the <u>weather/whether</u> is not great.
        (15)

Sometimes the temperature rises to 900°F! On those days, I'm not <u>aloud/allowed</u> to go outside.
        (16)

I just stay in and send e-mail to the rest of my <u>herd/heard</u> back on Earth. So now you know where
        (17)

I am. I hope you will send me some <u>mail/male</u> soon.
        (18)

Sincerely,

The Cow Who Jumped Over the Moon

Homophones

The Case of Fabulous Fritz

Jeremy Jenkins wrote this letter to his favorite author. He needs some help with homophones before he can send it, though. Can you help him?

Directions: *Homophones* are words that sound the same but have different spellings and different meanings. Circle the correct word in each pair of underlined words below.

Dear Mr. Glumpus,

I have never sent <u>mail/male</u> to an author before, but I
      (1)
had to let you <u>know/no</u> how much I love your book, *Fabulous*
      (2)
Fritz. Never before have I <u>red/read</u> about a dog like Fritz.
      (3)
I just got the book two <u>weaks/weeks</u> ago and have already memorized it. My favorite part
      (4)
is when Fritz pretends to be a rock star and everybody <u>stares/stairs</u> at him. You are <u>so/sew</u>
      (5)   (6)
creative! And when Fritz put peanut butter on his <u>nose/knows</u>, I thought I was going to <u>dye/die</u> of
      (7)   (8)
laughter. I, <u>to/too</u>, love peanut butter, though such antics are <u>not/knot</u> tolerated in my house.
      (9)   (10)
I am saving my allowance to <u>bye/buy</u> a <u>pair/pare</u> of Fabulous Fritz night-vision goggles.
      (11)   (12)
My <u>hole/whole</u> room is covered with Fritz stickers. And guess what I named my pet Burmese
      (13)
python? If you guessed "Fritz," <u>you're/your</u> correct. I <u>would/wood</u> change my name to Fritz, too,
      (14)   (15)
but my parents say I'm not <u>aloud/allowed</u>. I <u>heard/herd</u> that you <u>mite/might</u> <u>right/write</u> a 10-book
      (16)   (17)   (18)   (19)
series about Fritz. That <u>seems/seams</u> like a <u>great/grate</u> idea. I will never get <u>bored/board</u> with my
      (20)   (21)   (22)
favorite pooch.

Your #1 fan,

Jeremy Jenkins

Name: _____ Date: _____

Its/It's

The Case of the Big Bad Wolf

The wolf from "Little Red Riding Hood" is trying to tell his side of the story. But he doesn't really understand the difference between *its* and *it's*. Can you help?

Directions: The word *its* or *it's* belongs on each of the lines below. Choose the correct word and write it in.

I'm the wolf from "Little Red Riding Hood." You probably know me as the guy who ate Grandma. I'm here to tell you _____ all a big lie.

Every bedtime story needs _____ bad guy. But I didn't eat Grandma. I didn't dress up in Grandma's nightgown and chase Little Red Riding Hood. I didn't get killed by a hunter. _____ a big mistake.

_____ very simple. I was walking through the woods and I saw a basket with _____ lid open. I peeked inside and saw some cookies. I took just one cookie.

All of a sudden someone yelled, "Hey! Put that cookie back! _____ mine!"

I looked over and there was a little girl wearing a red cape and hood. She ran over and started yelling at me. She looked so scary! So I dropped the cookie. _____ crumbs flew behind me. I ran all the way home.

Little Red Riding Hood was so mad about her cookie. She started telling everyone that I had tried to eat her up. _____ all lies. You have to believe me. So the next time someone tells you the story of Little Red Riding Hood, tell my side of the story.

_____ the truth!

Grammar Cop's Clues

Remember these basic laws for *its* and *it's*:

- *It's* **is a contraction of** *it is* **or** *it has***. A contraction is made up of two words that are joined by an apostrophe. The apostrophe shows where one or more letters have been left out.**
(Example: *It's* time for lunch.)

- *Its* **is the possessive form of** *it* **(the fancy name is "possessive pronoun").** *Its* **shows that "it" owns something.** (Example: The squirrel dropped *its* acorn.)

Name: _____ **Date:** _____

Their/They're/There

The Case of the Worried Elf

Santa's head elf is worried. But he doesn't know the difference between _their_, _they're_, and _there_. Can you help him?

Directions: The word _their_, _they're_, or _there_ belongs on each of the lines below. Choose the correct word and write it in.

Dear Santa,

_____ is a problem with some of

the elves. _____ acting very lazy. I know that

Christmas isn't until the end of December, but the elves

aren't ready. Many of them don't have _____ tools

in shipshape. I caught a group of doll-making elves

playing with _____ Gameboys. I saw some of the

candy makers having a sword fight with _____

candy canes. I inspected _____ sleeping area and

I must tell you it's a disgusting mess down _____.

I found candy wrappers and soda cans everywhere.

      Santa, I know that the elves are a good bunch.

_____ all very sweet and nice. But _____

like a bunch of kids. We must ask them to improve

_____ work habits. We must make sure

_____ ready for the big day. We need to make them

responsible for cleaning all of _____ garbage. Most

of all, we must make them understand that _____

Santa's elves! Let's hope they get the message.

      Very sincerely,

      Rocko, your head elf

Grammar Cop's Clues

Remember these basic laws of _their_, _they're_, and _there_:

- **_Their_ is the possessive form of _they_. You use it when you want to say that something belongs to a group of people.** (Example: They went sledding, but they forgot _their_ mittens.)

- **_They're_ is a contraction of _they are_.** (Example: Mindy and Jessica are best friends. _They're_ always together.)

- **_There_ is a place. It is the opposite of _here_.** (Example: Australia is far away. I wonder if I'll ever go _there_.) **_There_ is also a pronoun used to introduce a sentence.** (Example: _There_ is someone at the door.)

Their/They're/There

The Case of the Stinky Dragon

Whoever wrote this advertisement doesn't know the difference between *their*, *there*, and *they're*. Can you help?

Directions: The word *their*, *there*, or *they're* belongs in each of the spaces below. Choose the correct word and write it in.

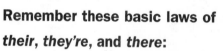

New, IMPROVED Dragon Breath!

The brand new mouthwash just for dragons

and _____ loved ones!

Finally, _____ is a new mouthwash for dragons and _____ families! Many dragons say _____ breath smells like a burnt hamburger. Some say _____ embarrassed when _____ breath causes _____ dentists to faint. But now _____ is a solution: new, improved Dragon Breath, the only mouthwash just for fire breathers. Dragons who use Dragon Breath find that _____ breath smells smoky fresh. _____ friends and families are thrilled. And _____ thrilled, too. So, try Dragon Breath! Or give a bottle to a dragon you love.

Grammar Cop's Clues

Remember these basic laws of *their*, *they're*, and *there*:

- *Their* is the possessive form of *they*. You use it when you want to say that something belongs to a group of people. (Example: They got *their* kiwis in New Zealand.)

- *They're* is a contraction of *they are*. (Example: If they live in New Zealand, *they're* called New Zealanders.)

- *There* is a place. It is the opposite of *here*. (Example: Aukland is the capital of New Zealand. I wonder if I'll ever go *there*.) *There* is also a pronoun used to introduce a sentence. (Example: *There* is nothing for me to do but wait.)

To/Too/Two

The Case of the Itsy Bitsy Spider

The Itsy Bitsy Spider wants to explain a few things, but he doesn't know the difference between *to*, *two*, and *too*. Can you help?

Directions: Write either *to*, *two*, or *too* on each blank below.

From the Desk of the Itsy Bitsy Spider

I'm the itsy bitsy spider and I need _____ set some things straight:

Number one: I'm not _____ itsy. I'm _____ inches long, and hairy, _____. If I landed on your shoulder, you'd jump nearly _____ the moon.

Number _____: I don't really like spending every day of my life climbing up that water spout. Just when I get _____ the top, down comes the rain and washes me _____ kingdom come. And then the sun comes out, dries up the rain, and bakes me like a Poptart. You think that's fun?

And then I have _____ get back up there and climb up _____ the top of that spout all over again. I wish I didn't have _____. I wish I could retire to the back of your sock drawer and eat a fly or _____. But you know what the song says. In the end, the itsy bitsy spider climbs up the spout again. So that's what I do. Otherwise, I'll be out of a job. Maybe you'd like to climb with me, _____.

Grammar Cop's Clues

Remember these basic laws of *to*, *too*, and *two*:

- ***To* is a preposition.** (Example: I returned the book *to* the library.) **Sometimes the word *to* also comes before a verb.** (Example: Lamont needs *to* pick up his younger brother.)

- ***Too* means "also" or "too much."** (Example: I have *too* much homework!)

- ***Two* is a number.** (Example: Linda was so hungry, she ate *two* huge hotdogs.)

Name: _____   **Date:** _____

To/Too/Two

The Case of the Surfing Elephant

Mr. Brandon L. Phant is looking for a new job. But he doesn't know the difference between *to*, *two*, and *too*. Can you help him?

Directions: Write the word *to*, *too*, or *two* in each of the blanks below.

The Hang Ten Surfboard Company

100 Enormous Wave Lane

Honolulu, Hawaii

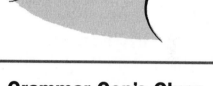

Dear Sirs and Madams,

    Allow me _____ introduce myself. My name is Brandon L. Phant. I am a _____-ton gray elephant and I believe I would make an ideal spokesperson for your surfboards. I came _____ Hawaii from South Africa, where I first learned _____ surf. My mother wasn't _____ thrilled when I began surfing. She said it was _____ dangerous. I told her _____ just relax. I move through the water like a graceful whale. I promised _____ wear a strong sunblock. I assured her that other surfers move out of the way when they see a _____-ton elephant riding a wave.

    I used _____ be a personal trainer, but I was _____ big for the Stairmaster. I'm interested in changing my career. My idea is that you hire me _____ be in commercials for your surfboards. I look great in a swimsuit. (Not _____ many elephants can say that!)

    I look forward _____ hearing from you!

              Sincerely,

              Brandon L. Phant

Grammar Cop's Clues

Remember these basic laws of *to*, *too*, and *two*:

- ***To* is a preposition.** (Example: I went *to* the doctor yesterday.) **Sometimes the word *to* also comes before a verb.** (Example: Before crossing the street, you need *to* look both ways.)

- ***Too* means "also" or "too much."** (Example: I'll join you for lunch. I'm feeling hungry, *too*.)

- ***Two* is a number.** (Example: Those *two* cats were making too much noise last night.)

Name: _____   Date: _____

Your/You're

The Education of Snow White

Snow White has left the seven dwarfs' cottage. She wants to explain her disappearance, but she doesn't really understand the difference between *your* and *you're*. Can you help her fill in the blanks?

Directions: The word *your* or *you're* belongs on each of the lines below. Choose the correct word and write it in.

Dear Dwarfs,

_____ probably wondering why I left. I have to admit, I have gotten tired of _____ strange habits. It seems like if _____ not sneezing, then _____ sleeping, or _____ acting grumpy.

Also, it turned out the prince wasn't for me. As I said to him, "_____ really nice, but I don't want to sit around _____ castle all day while _____ off slaying dragons."

The other day, I took a good look in the mirror. Sure it said, "_____ the fairest of them all." But it also said, "Plan for _____ future. What about _____ education? _____ career?"

That was it. "Snow," I said, "say good-bye to _____ dwarfs. _____ going back to school."

I hope I haven't hurt _____ little feelings. I appreciate _____ kindness. _____ all very generous. But for now, _____ on _____ own.

_____ friend,
Snow White

Grammar Cop's Clues

Remember these basic laws of *your* and *you're*:

- *Your* **is the possessive form of** *you*. **Use it when you are talking about something that belongs to the person with whom you are speaking.**
(Example: I really like *your* new jeans. Where did you get them?)

- *You're* **is a contraction of** *you are*. **Here's a tip: Whenever you write** *you're*, **read over the sentence again and substitute the words** *you are* **for** *you're*. **If the sentence makes sense, you've made the right choice.**
(Example: I always tell people that *you're* the best dancer in our grade.)

Your/You're

The Case of the Unemployed Princess

Sleeping Beauty wrote this letter to the Royal Mattress Company. But she doesn't understand the difference between *your* and *you're*. Can you help?

Directions: The word *your* or *you're* belongs on each of the lines below. Choose the correct word and write it in.

From the Desk of Sleeping Beauty

The Royal Mattress Company
29 Goose Feather Lane
Wunsuhponna Kingdom

To Whom It May Concern:

_____ not going to believe this. I've been asleep for one hundred years on one of _____ mattresses! And I feel great! I've been telling everyone how terrific _____ beds are.

Is _____ company looking for a spokesperson? I'd be perfect. After all, I have tons of sleeping experience! If _____ interested, I could come to _____ factory and test _____ new mattresses. Just think what a good word from me could do for _____ company.

_____ probably saying to yourselves, "Hire a princess? Never!" Well, _____ wrong. Times have changed since I fell asleep. I just woke up an hour ago, and a handsome prince said to me, "I want to marry you. But _____ going to have to get a job." So I sat right down to write this letter.

_____ welcome to contact me at the palace. I look forward to _____ reply.

_____ biggest fan,
Sleeping Beauty

Grammar Cop's Clues

Remember these basic laws of *your* and *you're*:

- ***Your* is the possessive form of *you*. Use it when you are talking about something that belongs to the person with whom you are speaking.**
  (Example: You dropped *your* bag.)

- ***You're* is a contraction of *you are*. Here's a tip: Whenever you write *you're*, read over the sentence again and substitute the words *you are* for *you're*. If the sentence makes sense, you've made the right choice.**
  (Example: *You're* so busy, I hardly see you anymore.)

Your/You're

The Case of the Slimy Aliens

The slimy aliens from the planet Gooeygoopiter need to read this important advertisement. Can you help the writer fill in the blanks?

Directions: Write either *your* or *you're* on each blank.

If _____ an alien from the planet Gooeygoopiter, listen up!

Do you have an embarrassing slime problem? Does it positively ooze from _____ ears and toes? Do _____ feet leave embarrassing gooey marks on the carpets of _____ human friends?

_____ in for a wonderful surprise. _____ problems are about to be solved with SLIME AWAY, the first slime remover especially engineered for _____ embarrassing problem. Here is how SLIME AWAY will change _____ life. Simply apply it to _____ toes and ears. Wait five minutes. Then watch as SLIME AWAY works. Like magic!

_____ going to be amazed.

Never again will you have to wear slime-catching buckets on _____ears. Never again will you have to pay _____ friends' carpet-cleaning bills. Never again will you hear _____ friends whisper, "Uh-oh, here comes the slime machine" as _____ walking through their door. _____ problem will disappear—and so will _____ worries.

_____ only moments away from relief.

SLIME AWAY! $49.00 plus tax.

Grammar Cop's Clues

Remember these basic laws of *your* and *you're*:

- ***Your* is the possessive form of *you*. Use it when you are talking about something that belongs to the person with whom you are speaking.** (Example: I promise I'll return *your* CD tomorrow.)

- ***You're* is a contraction of *you are*. Here's a tip: Whenever you write *you're*, read over the sentence again and substitute the words *you are* for *you're*. If the sentence makes sense, you've made the right choice.** (Example: *You're* really such a good friend.)

Name: _____ **Date:** _____

Your/You're

The Case of the Sad Spider

This spider needs some help before he can send this note to Miss Muffet. He is confused about how to use *your* and *you're*.

Directions: Write either *your* or *you're* on each blank below.

Dear Miss Muffet,

I'm sorry. I didn't mean to scare you, honest. I just wanted to be _____ friend! All I did was sit down beside you and . . . well, it doesn't matter now. _____ gone.

Listen, this is a bit awkward, but I need to talk to you about _____ dish of curds and whey. You left it sitting here by _____ tuffet. I was thinking that if _____ not going to eat it, maybe I could. It's _____ call, though! If you want the curds, the whey, or both, just let me know!

You don't have to tell me _____ reasons for leaving. Maybe _____ shy. Maybe _____ used to eating alone. Maybe spiders just aren't _____ thing. It's _____ business, not mine. But honey, I need to know what to do with _____ food.

Respectfully,

A. Spider

Grammar Cop's Clues
Remember these basic laws of *your* and *you're*:

• ***Your* is the possessive form of *you*. Use it when you are talking about something that belongs to the person with whom you are speaking.**
(Example: It's *your* turn to wash the dishes tonight.)

• ***You're* is a contraction of *you are*. Here's a tip: Whenever you write *you're*, read over the sentence again and substitute *you are* for *you're*. If the sentence makes sense, you've made the right choice.** (Example: They say *you're* a singer, too.)

Name: _____   Date: _____

Your/You're, Its/It's

The Case of the Dissatisfied Dog

Poochie Doodle wants a new doghouse and has written this letter to his family. Problem is, he doesn't know when to use *your* or *you're* and *its* or *it's*. (Big surprise!) Can you help him?

Directions: On each underline, write either *your* or *you're*. Inside each box, write either *its* or *it's*.

Dear Family,

    As _____ aware, I have been _____ loyal dog for five happy years. _____ great people, and [ ] always been a pleasure being _____ dog. That's why what I'm about to say is difficult for me. But I think [ ] important, so here it goes.

    I hate the doghouse you built for me. [ ] too small and [ ] design is not practical. I have nowhere to entertain and nowhere to store my toys. Plus, [ ] not safe! There is no lock, let alone an alarm system. Perhaps _____ not aware of this, but the skunks in this neighborhood are looking for a new clubhouse!

    I hope _____ not offended, but I have hired an architect to draw up some plans for a new house. _____ going to love her work! She designed the house of the star of Air Bud. ([ ] pictured in the latest issue of *Dog Fancy*, if you want to see it.) The new house will be a great addition to _____ property, I promise. So whenever [ ] convenient, let's get together and talk.

                   _____ pet,
                   Poochie Doodles

Grammar Cop's Clues

Remember these basic rules:

- ***Your* is the possessive form of *you*. Use it when you are talking about something that belongs to the person with whom you are speaking.** (Example: Can I borrow *your* bat during practice?)

- ***You're* is a contraction of *you are*. Whenever you write *you're*, read over the sentence again and substitute *you are* for *you're*. If the sentence makes sense, you've made the right choice.** (Example: So *you're* the one who won.)

- ***It's* is a contraction of *it is* or *it has*.** (Example: *It's* going to start raining soon.)

- ***Its* is the possessive form of *it* (the fancy name is "possessive pronoun"). *Its* shows that "it" owns something.** (Example: The dog buried *its* bone in the backyard.)

Answers

The Case of the Strange Playground Equipment (p. 7)
> **Nouns:** company; letter; one; roller coaster; school; backyard; opportunity; plans; letter; shame; crayon; ideas; picture; loop; cook; cafeteria; roller coaster; name; suggestion; kids; thing; spelling; signature; kid; R's; education; reading; writing; rides; water parks; manager. **Proper Nouns:** Principal Billsley; Super-Riders Construction Team; "Kara Has Cooties Coaster;" "Multiplication Shocker;" "Research Report Terror;" Pickens Elementary; Tim Showtime

The Case of Rapunzel's Long Hair (p. 8)
> **Nouns:** hair; hairdresser; boys; jobs; door; name; witch; tower; stairs; hair; ladder; hair; witch; locks; feet; hair; bottle; week; expense; room; problem; date; ball; hair; boots; feet; boys; women; style; hair; shoulders; dancers. **Proper Nouns:** Hair Innovations; Royal Ball; Cute Clips; Fine Styles; Rapunzel; Wanda; Fairytale Shampoo; Prince Charming; King Phillip; Rapunzel

The Case of Jack and Jill (p. 9)
> him; he; He; he; him; he; He; he; He; him; he; He; him; He; him; him; he; he

The Case of the Old Woman in the Shoe (p. 10)
> me; I; I; I; me; I; I; I; me; me; I; I; me; I; me

The Case of a Letter to Old MacDonald (p. 11)
> 1. we 2. we 3. We 4. We 5. us 6. us 7. We 8. us 9. we 10. We

The Case of the Bumbling Cupids (p. 12)
> 1. Cupids 2. skies 3. arrows 4. couples 5. mistakes 6. disasters 7. tips 8. landings 9. roofs 10. bushes 11. mailboxes 12. points 13. glasses 14. flies 15. eyes

The Apology of Goldilocks (p. 13)
> guys; germs; everyone's; Baby Bear's; bears'; woods; rocks; jumper's; Baby Bear's; rocks'; family's; parents'

The Case of Mary Had a Little Rooster (p. 14)
> 1. heard 2. gets 3. sing 4. am 5. thinks 6. likes 7 heard 8. try 9. tried 10. did 11. fell 12. sent 13. give 14. heard 15. write

The Case of the Dog Who Eats Homework (p. 15)
> 1. want 2. comes 3. ask 4. replies 5. has 6. confess 7. eat 8. travel 9. get 10. like 11. is 12. was 13. shows 14. typed

The Case of the Cat Food Casserole (p. 16)
> happened; sliced; chopped; cooked; rang; whispered; talked; watched; said; grabbed; dumped; mixed; stuck; loved; felt; was; asked; opened; did; saw; was; emptied; ate; hurt

The Case of the Saxophone Disaster (p. 17)
> **Adjectives:** little; big; whole; last; dear; cozy; messy; right; crazy; pepperoni; fuzzy; purple; poor; pepperoni; little; green; front; serious; next; American; sorry. **Adverbs:** suddenly; thoroughly; repeatedly; ridiculously; never; happily; eventually; Again; Suddenly; loudly; quickly; angrily

The Case of the Unexpected Delay (p. 18)
> **Adjectives:** bad; big; gingerbread; strange; coconut; sticky; giant; normal; new; loyal; unusual; big; excited; first; purple; giant; short; huge; red; inside; favorite; sick; Heavy; seventeen; Chubby; chubby; graham-cracker; more; physical; wonderful. **Adverbs:** originally; humbly; joyfully; especially; anxiously; faster; nearly; regularly; Suddenly; professionally; quickly; Sincerely

the case of the missing capital letters (p. 19)
> Cinderella; There; The; I; I'm; I; I; I; Are; Disney; World; I; Anyway; Florida; So; Cinderella; I; If; I; They

The Case of the Fairy Godmother for Hire (p. 20)
> Molly; Street; York; Dear; the; My; me; she; Luckyfellow; Disney; World; I; Palm; Florida; I; *Vegetables*; April; Beauty; Sincerely

The Case of Freddy's Tarantula (p. 21)
> (1) Mom (2) Dad (4) Mom (6) Aunt (7) Mom (9) Grandma (12) Uncle (13) Mom (15) Dad

The Case of Frosty's Rules (p. 22)
> Dear; Fellow; Snowmen; Snowwomen; It's; To; I; Don't; I; No; Have; Do; I; Minnesota; Vikings; Buffalo; Bills; No; Last; Julius; Iceman; Minneapolis; Police; Department; *How*; *Grinch*; *Stole*; *Christmas*; Melville; He; Do; Gameboy; Do; I; There; I; If; Stop; Shop; Sincerely; Frosty

The Case of Humpty Dumpty (p. 23)
> 2. don't 3. You're 4. shouldn't 5. Don't 6. aren't 7. can't 8. don't 9. I'm 10. couldn't 11. It's 12. I'll

The Case of the Grumpy Goose (p. 24)
> 2. doesn't 3. somebody's 4. can't 5. it's 6. I'd 7. couldn't 8. don't 9. you're 10. wouldn't 11. I'll 12. aren't 13. I've

The Case of the Sick Bookworm (p. 25)
> 2. I'm 3. I've 4. I'd 5. couldn't 6. she'll 7. can't 8. you're 9. don't 10. it's 11. doesn't 12. you'll

The Case of the Chicken That Crossed the Road (p. 26)
> 2. haven't 3. You're 4. aren't 5. I'm 6. I'll 7. don't 8. I've 9. It's 10. you've 11. Isn't 12. here's 13. I'd 14. We'd 15. That's 16. won't 17. You'll

The Case of the Wanna-be Superstar (p. 27)
> Dear Mom and Dad,
>
> I'm going to be a star! I saw an ad for Starmakers in the back of a comic book. For two years, they have made their name by turning youngsters like me into pop music idols—overnight! I just need $1,000 for their how-to book. Can I have a loan?
>
> If I'm going to become a superstar, I'll need a new hairstyle. A neon green mohawk will look great on stage. Also, you'll need to buy a limousine. I can't bear having you pick me up from school in the minivan anymore! It doesn't fit my new image. I just know crowds will come every night to hear me sing. I have real talent. After all these years of listening to me in the shower, you must know that I'm great. Even Bubba loves howling along to my version of "The Star-Spangled Banner."
>
> I'll sell millions of records! You'll see my picture in hundreds of magazines. This could be my big break! So, can I have

the $1,000? Of course, I'll pay you back when I become a multi-millionaire. I'll save every cent, honest. Please don't say no. Do you think the principal would excuse me from school for a world tour with Avril?

Your son,

Billy

The Case of the Weary Lunch Lady (p. 28)

Dear Lunch Lady Ruth,

Lately we students have noticed that you seem overworked. You look tired. Your hairnet is always on crooked. You can barely keep your eyes open as we slide our trays by you. Once you dumped a ladleful of gravy on Tommy's head! His mom was not pleased when she got the dry-cleaning bill for his Boy Scout uniform.

It can't be easy to feed all of us. It must take hours of chopping broccoli, slicing brussels sprouts, and cooking lima beans to fix lunch for hundreds of students. Things need to change! Don't get us wrong. We appreciated the liver meatballs you fixed for us last Thursday. Just because that food fight started before we could eat any of them doesn't mean we wouldn't have loved the meal. Those meatballs were just so easy to throw! They bounced nicely, too. Oh, and sorry you had to clean up the cafeteria afterwards. Still, it was pretty impressive how high we got those spaghetti noodles stuck up on the wall, wasn't it?

Let us make a suggestion. Candy Corn and Jelly Beans require absolutely no preparation in the kitchen. Just grab a bunch, set them on the plate, and hand them to us hungry students. We'll be happy to put them in our stomachs, not on each other. Can Swedish Fish provide us with protein? Candy Corn is a vegetable, right?

We hope you will consider our proposal.

Sincerely,

The Students of Webster Elementary

The Three Little Pigs' Day in Court (p. 29)

"I hate to be a pig," Daisy said, "but I think we should sue him."

"What's the problem?" asked the judge.

"Wolf won't leave us alone," said Hambone. "He keeps blowing down our houses."

Porky said, "He turned my house into a pigsty!"

"They're all hogwash," said Wolf. "I'm not guilty."

"Do you have witnesses?" he asked the pigs.

"I saw everything," she said. "The pigs are telling the truth. Wolf is a real beast!"

"What a relief," Daisy said. "Maybe now we'll all live happily ever after!"

The Case of the Frog Prince (p. 30)

writing; disappointed; refused; turn; apologized; again; comment; enough; very; wrecking; terrible; although; delicious; palace; afraid; college; doubt; reconsider; where; right

The Case of the Careless Typist (p. 31)

reading; write; pieces; their; favorite; understand; fascinated; different; interesting; where; advice; discover; secret; guess

The Case of the Terrible Tooth Fairy (p. 32)

received; kitchen; whipped; sandwich; Afterwards; dancing; screaming; nearly; heard; quietly; carefully; believe; problem; another; understand

The Case of the Missing Rabbit (p. 33)

(2) variety (4) weird (6) cashier (7) their (8) believe (9) Neither (11) thief (13) field

The Case of Frosty the Snowman (p. 34)

1. know 2. soul 3. see 4. made 5. know 6. through 7. wear 8. nose 9. sense 10. flew 11. hour 12. know 13. there 14. threw

The Case of the Cow Who Jumped Over the Moon (p. 35)

1. know 2. stationery 3. write 4. through 5. way 6. where 7. one 8. bears 9. see 10. meet 11. week 12. here 13. to 14. sun 15. weather 16. allowed 17. herd 18. mail

The Case of the Fabulous Fritz (p. 36)

1. mail 2. know 3. read 4. weeks 5. stares 6. so 7. nose 8. die 9. too 10. not 11. buy 12. pair 13. whole 14. you're 15. would 16. allowed 17. heard 18. might 19. write 20. seems 21. great 22. bored

The Case of the Big Bad Wolf (p. 37)

it's; its; It's; It's; its; It's; Its; It's; It's

The Case of the Worried Elf (p. 38)

There; They're; their; their; their; their; there; They're; they're; their; they're; their; they're

The Case of the Stinky Dragon (p. 39)

their; there; their; their; they're; their; their; there; their; Their; they're

The Case of the Itsy Bitsy Spider (p. 40)

to; too; two; too; to; two; to; to; to; to; to; two; too

The Case of the Surfing Elephant (p. 41)

to; two; to; to; too; too; to; to; two; to; too; to; too; to

The Education of Snow White (p. 42)

You're; your; you're; you're; you're; You're; your; you're; You're; your; your; Your; your; You're; your; your; You're; you're; your; Your

The Case of the Unemployed Princess (p. 43)

You're; your; your; your; you're; your; your; your; You're; you're; you're; You're; your; Your

The Case of the Slimy Aliens (p. 44)

you're; your; your; your; You're; Your; your; your; You're; your; your; your; you're; Your; your; You're

The Case of the Sad Spider (p. 45)

your; You're; your; your; you're; your; your; you're; you're; your; your; your

The Case of the Dissatisfied Dog (p. 46)

you're; your; You're; it's your; it's; It's; its; it's; you're; you're; You're; It's; your; it's; Your